TCM 2765

Dr. Fry's
Vocabulary
Fun
Intermediate

by Edward Fry, Ph.D.

Teacher Created Materials, Inc.

Ollie Huddleston

Vocabulary Fun

Grades 4–8

by Edward Fry, Ph.D.
Professor Emeritus
Rutgers University

Editor
Eric Migliaccio

Teacher Created Materials, Inc.
6421 Industry Way
Westminster, CA 92683
www.teachercreated.com

ISBN-1-57690-765-1

©2000 Revised by Teacher Created Materials, Inc.
Reprinted, 2002

Made in U.S.A.

Table of Contents

Introduction

Words make a lot of difference. Good writers use interesting words. They have large and varied vocabularies. Good readers know the meanings behind lots of words.

Many types of tests use vocabulary as one of their chief assessment areas. State standardized tests and national tests nearly always assess vocabulary one way or another. It might not always be called a "vocabulary" section, but you can score poorly in "comprehension" or "word usage" if there are many words which you don't know.

The well-known tests, like the College Board and other examinations for entering college or professional schools, often rely heavily on vocabulary knowledge. While this book is aimed well below the college entrance level, one of the purposes of this book is to begin to build an interest in words.

Building a vocabulary is a lifelong task. It begins in the home and in the crib. It must be reinforced at every stage—kindergarten, elementary school, secondary school, and even for senior citizens. Certainly one of the reasons for failure in secondary and college courses is lack of knowledge of the vocabulary used in that subject.

This book will teach some vocabulary, but its real purpose is to awaken a deeper interest in words—all kinds of words: portmanteau words (the words that are all scrunched together like "motel"), clipped words (for example, "gym" for "gymnasium"), abbreviations (like "MO" for "Missouri"), and origins of the days of the week (like "Moon's Day" for "Monday").

Don't hesitate to extend these lessons further by discussing similar words. Try to get them into use by your students in both speaking and writing practice. Above all, help to develop an interest in every kind of vocabulary from slang in dialogue to formal words in essays, in subjects such as mathematics or social studies, and in just plain everyday use.

Name _____ Date _____

Lesson 1a: Clipped Words

Directions: "Clipped" (or shortened) words are words we use all the time.

If "flu" is the clipped word for "influenza" and "gas" is the clipped word for "gasoline," what is the clipped word for the following words?

You can select your answer from the Answer Box below.

1. telephone_____

2. necktie_____

3. bicycle _____

4. submarine _____

5. airplane _____

6. luncheon _____

7. moving picture_____

8. veterinarian _____

9. zoological garden _____

10. limousine _____

Answer Box

limo	lunch	movie
market	typo	cab
burger	exam	tails
trig	bike	vet
zoo	phone	cuke
dorm	stat	sub
plane	tie	

Name _____ Date _____

Lesson 1b: More Clipped Words

Directions: Here are some clipped words.

What is the full word for these words?

Example: vet = veterinarian

You can select your answer from the Answer Box below.

1. ad _____

2. auto _____

3. memo _____

4. con_____

5. taxi_____

6. teen _____

7. gym _____

8. math _____

9. pop _____

10. photo _____

Answer Box

market	mathematics	professor
penitentiary	graduate	teenager
automobile	advertisement	graduate
helicopter	stereophonic	popular
mathematics	taxicab	convict
memorandum	percolate	gymnasium
photograph	caravan	

Name _____ Date _____

Lesson 2a: Portmanteau Words

Directions: Portmanteau words are words that have been blended together. Write the word that has been blended.

Example: smoke + fog = smog

You can select your answer from the Answer Box below.

1. binary + digit _____

2. breakfast + lunch_____

3. flash + gush_____

4. God + be (with) + ye _____

5. modulator + demodulator _____

6. motor + pedal _____

7. motor + hotel_____

8. picture + element _____

9. television + marathon _____

10. twist + whirl _____

Answer Box

modem	pixel	twirl
motel	blimp	blotch
bleep	brunch	goodbye
flush	chortle	clash
clump	con man	farewell
gerrymander	glimmer	bit
moped	telethon	

Name _____ Date _____

Lesson 2b: More Portmanteau Words

Directions: Write the two words that have been blended.

Example: television + marathon = telethon

You can select your answer from the Answer Box below.

1. daisy _____

2. flare _____

3. smash _____

4. fortnight _____

5. hi-fi _____

6. o'clock _____

7. Skylab _____

8. travelogue _____

9. flurry _____

10. motorcade _____

Answer Box

fare + ye + well	smoke + fog	travel + monologue
sky + laboratory	day's + eye	high + fidelity
of (the) + clock	fourteen + nights	motor + cavalcade
flame + glare	flutter + hurry	by + cause
smack + mash	parachute + troops	

Name _____ Date _____

Lesson 3a: Acronyms and Abbreviations

Directions: Acronyms and abbreviations are used frequently in everyday communication. Write the acronym or abbreviation for the following words.

Example: We frequently write and say the abbreviation "U.S." meaning "United States."

You can select your answer from the Answer Box below.

1. American Broadcasting Company _____

2. Acquired Immune Deficiency Syndrome _____

3. Cash on delivery _____

4. Disc jockey _____

5. District Attorney _____

6. Intelligent Quotient _____

7. Internal Revenue Service _____

8. Mind your own business _____

9. North Atlantic Treaty Organization _____

10. Recreational vehicle _____

Answer Box

SNAFU	ROTC	DJ
COBOL	ASAP	ABC
DA	IQ	MIA
AIDS	COD	RV
CPA	WASP	MYOB
SOS	IRS	
NATO	NABISCO	

Name _____ Date _____

Lesson 3b: More Acronyms and Abbreviations

Directions: Here are some acronyms and abbreviations. Write the words for the initials.

Example: "DOA" stands for "dead on arrival."

You can select your answer from the Answer Box below.

1. PS _____

2. RR _____

3. RSVP_____

4. SCUBA _____

5. TV _____

6. UFO_____

7. UNESCO_____

8. VIP_____

9. ZIP_____

10. NAACP _____

Answer Box

television

tender loving care

special weapons action team

modus operandi

respondez s'il vous plait

postscript

unidentified flying object

vice president

zone improvement plan

women's army corps

self-contained underwater breathing apparatus

radio detecting and ranging

public address

United Nations Educational, Scientific, and Cultural Organization

railroad

very important person

National Association for the Advancement of Colored People

Name _____ Date _____

Lesson 4a: Words Coined from People's Names

Directions: Many of our words come from the name of the person who discovered, invented, or is associated with something. Choose the word associated with the famous name.

Example: The electricity unit "volt" is named after the Italian physicist Alessandro Volata.

You can select your answer from the box below.

1. Jules Leotard _____

2. John Stetson _____

3. John Montagu, fourth Earl of Sandwich _____

4. Frederick Mesmer _____

5. Ambrose Burnside _____

6. Samuel Maverick _____

7. Louis Pasteur _____

8. Amelia Bloomer _____

9. Etienne de Silhouette _____

10. Nicholas Chauvin _____

Answer Box

cardigan	silhouette	pasteurize
dunce	fahrenheit	leotard
sandwich	stetson	mesmerize
maverick	bloomers	volt
vandal	sequoia	chauvinist
sideburns		

Name _____ Date _____

Lesson 4b: More Words Coined from People's Names

Directions: Here are some words that came from people's names. Select the person's name associated with the word.

Example: French physicist Andre Ampere gave us "ampere," or "amp," which is the basic measure of an electric current.

Use the Answer Box below to help you find the right word.

1. America _____

2. frisbee _____

3. Braille _____

4. teddy bear _____

5. valentine _____

6. Ferris wheel_____

7. diesel_____

8. Adam's apple_____

9. nicotine _____

10. saxophone_____

Answer Box

James Bowie	Teddy Roosevelt	Anton Sax
Elbridge Gerry	Captain Fudge	William Frisbie
Sir Francis Beaufort	Sylvester Graham	Rudolf Diesel
Louis Braille	Charles Boycott	Amerigo Vespucci
G. M. Ferris	Adam	Andre Ampere
James Watt	St. Valentine	Jean Nicot
Jean Baudot	Ernst Mach	Alexander Bell

Review Quizzes

You can look back at the lesson if you are stuck or can't spell the words correctly, but first try to give the answer without looking back.

Lesson 1a Review: Clipped Words
What is the full word for these words?

Example: vet = veterinarian

1. teen _____

2. gym _____

3. math _____

4. pop _____

5. photo _____

6. ad _____

7. auto _____

8. memo _____

9. con_____

10. taxi_____

- -

Lesson 1b Review: More Clipped Words

If "flu" is the clipped word for "influenza" and "gas" is the clipped word for "gasoline," what is the clipped word for each of these words?

1. luncheon _____

2. moving picture_____

3. veterinarian _____

4. zoological garden _____

5. limousine _____

6. telephone_____

7. necktie_____

8. bicycle _____

9. submarine _____

10. airplane _____

Review Quizzes *(cont.)*

You can look back at the lesson if you are stuck or can't spell the words correctly, but first try to give the answer without looking back.

Lesson 2a Review: Portmanteau Words

What are the two words that have been blended?

Example: "Smog" is the blend of "smoke" and "fog."

1. o'clock _____

2. Skylab _____

3. travelogue _____

4. flurry _____

5. motorcade _____

6. daisy _____

7. flare _____

8. smash _____

9. fortnight _____

10. hi-fi _____

- -

Lesson 2b Review: More Portmanteau Words

What is the word that is the blend of the two words?

Example: television + marathon = telethon

1. motor + pedal _____

2. motor + hotel _____

3. picture + element _____

4. television + marathon _____

5. twist + whirl _____

6. binary + digit _____

7. breakfast + lunch _____

8. flash + gush _____

9. God + be (with) + ye _____

10. modulator + demodulator _____

Review Quizzes *(cont.)*

You can look back at the lesson if you are stuck or can't spell the words correctly, but first try to give the answer without looking back.

Lesson 3a Review: Acronyms and Abbreviations

What do these acronyms stand for?

Example: We frequently write the abbreviation "U.S." for "United States."

1. UFO _____

2. UNESCO _____

3. VIP _____

4. ZIP _____

5. NAACP _____

6. PS_____

7. RR _____

8. RSVP _____

9. SCUBA _____

10. TV_____

- -

Lesson 3b Review: More Acronyms and Abbreviations

What are the acronyms or abbreviations for the following terms.

Example: "Dead on arrival" would be "DOA."

1. American Broadcasting Company _____

2. Acquired Immune Deficiency Syndrome _____

3. Cash on delivery_____

4. Disc jockey _____

5. District Attorney _____

6. Intelligence quotient _____

7. Internal Revenue Service_____

8. Mind your own business_____

9. North Atlantic Treaty Organization _____

10. Recreational vehicle _____

Review Quizzes *(cont.)*

You can look back at the lesson if you are stuck or can't spell the words correctly, but first try to give the answer without looking back.

Lesson 4a Review: Words Coined from People's Names

Write the word that comes from each person's name in the list below.

Example: The electricity unit "volt" is named after the Italian physicist Allesandro Volata.

1. Samuel Maverick _____

2. Louis Pasteur _____

3. Amelia Bloomer _____

4. Etienne de Silhouette _____

5. Nicholas Chauvin _____

6. Jules Leotard _____

7. John Stetson _____

8. John Montagu, fourth Earl of Sandwich _____

9. Frederick Mesmer_____

10. Ambrose Burnside _____

- -

Lesson 4b Review: More Words Coined from People's Names

Write the name of the person who discovered, invented, or is associated with the words in the following list.

Example: French physicist Andre Ampere gave us "ampere," which is the basic measure of an electric current.

1. Ferris wheel_____
2. diesel_____
3. Adam's apple_____
4. nicotine _____
5. saxophone_____

6. America_____
7. frisbee _____
8. Braille _____
9. teddy bear _____
10. valentine _____

Answer Key

Lesson 1

A: Clipped Words (page 4)

1. phone
2. tie
3. bike
4. sub
5. plane
6. lunch
7. movie
8. vet
9. zoo
10. limo

B: More Clipped Words (page 5)

1. advertisement
2. automobile
3. memorandum
4. convict
5. taxicab
6. teenager
7. gymnasium
8. mathematics
9. popular
10. photograph

Lesson 2

A: Portmanteau Words (page 6)

1. bit
2. brunch
3. flush
4. goodbye
5. modem
6. moped
7. motel
8. pixel
9. telethon
10. twirl

B: More Portmanteau Words (page 7)

1. day's + eye
2. flame + glare
3. smack + mash
4. fourteen + nights
5. high + fidelity
6. of (the) clock
7. sky + laboratory
8. travel + monologue
9. flutter + hurry
10. motor + cavalcade

Lesson 3

A: Acronyms and Abbreviations (page 8)

1. ABC
2. AIDS
3. COD
4. DJ
5. DA
6. IQ
7. IRS
8. MYOB
9. NATO
10. RV

B: More Acronyms and Abbreviations (page 9)

1. postscript
2. railroad
3. respondez s'il vous plait
4. self-contained underwater breathing apparatus
5. television
6. unidentified flying object
7. United Nations Educational, Scientific, and Cultural Organization
8. very important person
9. zone improvement plan
10. National Association for the Advancement of Colored People

Lesson 4

A: Words Coined from People's Names (page 10)

1. leotard
2. stetson
3. sandwich
4. mesmerize
5. sideburns
6. maverick
7. pasteurize
8. bloomers
9. silhouette
10. chauvinist

B: More Words Coined from People's Names (page 11)

1. Amerigo Vespucci
2. William Frisbie
3. Louis Braille
4. Teddy Roosevelt
5. St. Valentine
6. G. M. Ferris
7. Rudolf Diesel
8. Adam
9. Jean Nicot
10. Anton Sax

Answer Key *(cont.)*

Lesson 1 Review

A: Clipped Words (page 12)

1. teenager
2. gymnasium
3. mathematics
4. popular
5. photograph
6. advertisement
7. automobile
8. memorandum
9. convict
10. taxicab

B: More Clipped Words (page 12)

1. lunch
2. movie
3. vet
4. zoo
5. limo
6. phone
7. tie
8. bike
9. sub
10. plane

Lesson 2 Review

A: Portmanteau Words (page 13)

1. of (the) clock
2. sky + laboratory
3. travel + monologue
4. flutter + hurry
5. motor + cavalcade
6. day's + eye
7. flame + glare
8. smack + mash
9. fourteen + nights
10. high + fidelity

B: More Portmanteau Words (page 13)

1. moped
2. motel
3. pixel
4. telethon
5. twirl
6. bit
7. brunch
8. flush
9. goodbye
10. modem

Lesson 3 Review

A: Acronyms and Abbreviations (page 14)

1. unidentified flying object
2. United Nations Educational, Scientific, and Cultural Organization
3. very important person
4. zone improvement plan
5. National Association for the Advancement of Colored People
6. postscript
7. railroad
8. respondez s'il vous plait
9. self-contained underwater breathing apparatus
10. television

B: More Acronyms and Abbreviations (page 14)

1. ABC
2. AIDS
3. COD
4. DJ
5. DA
6. IQ
7. IRS
8. MYOB
9. NATO
10. RV

Lesson 4 Review

A: Words Coined from People's Names (page 15)

1. maverick
2. pasteurize
3. bloomers
4. silhouette
5. chauvinist
6. leotard
7. stetson
8. sandwich
9. mesmerize
10. sideburns

B: More Words Coined from People's Names (page 15)

1. G. M. Ferris
2. Rudolf Diesel
3. Adam
4. Jean Nicot
5. Anton Sax
6. Amerigo Vespucci
7. William Frisbie
8. Louis Braille
9. Teddy Roosevelt
10. St. Valentine

Name _____ Date _____

Lesson 5a: Calendar Words

Directions: Greek, Roman, and Norse/Teutonic mythology give us many words that have been assimilated into our everyday language. The examples below particularly relate to the calendar, the days of the week, and the months of the year. Pick the term taken from the ancients that we use today.

Example: Ceres, a Roman goddess of agriculture, gives us the word we use today to request what can be part of our morning meal, "cereal."

Use the Answer Box below to help you find the right word.

1. Tiw's day _____

2. The moon's day_____

3. Saturn's day _____

4. The sun's day _____

5. Julius Caesar_____

6. Octo (eight) _____

7. Decem (ten) _____

8. Aprilis (opening) _____

9. Mars, god of war _____

10. Juno, goddess of marriage _____

Answer Box

Saturday	March	echo
Sunday	April	December
cereal	Achilles	atlas
Orcus	Amazon	Vulcan
November	Tuesday	June
Eros	Oedipus	October
Monday	July	

Name _____ Date _____

Lesson 5b: More Calendar Words

Directions: Write is the Greek, Roman, or Norse/Teutonic origin for the following calendar words?

Example: Vulcan, the Roman god of fire, gives us the word "volcano."

1. July _____

2. Wednesday _____

3. Friday _____

4. Thursday _____

5. November _____

6. August _____

7. May _____

8. January _____

9. September _____

10. February _____

Answer Box

Orcus (Roman god of Underworld)	**Augustus Caesar** (Roman emperor)	**Achilles** (Greek warrior)
februa (Roman feast)	**Eros** (Greek god of love)	**Oedipus** (Greek king)
novem (Latin for "nine")	**Thor's day** (Norse god)	**Janus** (god with two faces)
Woden's day (Norse god)	**Maia** (Roman goddess)	**Ceres** (agriculture goddess)
septem (Latin for "seven")	**Fria's day** (Norse goddess)	**Julius Caesar** (Roman general)

Name _____ Date _____

Lesson 6a: Contractions

Contractions are two words blended together, with part of the second word omitted. We often use contractions in speech, but less often in writing. They are regularly used in writing down speech (for example, Sally said, "You're my best friend.").

Here are most of the contraction types you'll see:

'm = am	I'm very happy.	(I'm = I am)
're = are	You're very happy.	(you're = you are)
's = is	She's very happy.	(she's = she is)
'd = would	He'd do it for you.	(he'd = he would)
've = have	We've all been there.	(we've = we have)
'll = will	I'll do it tomorrow.	(I'll = I will)
n't = not	Don't walk fast.	(don't = do not)

Directions: Write out the full meaning of the following contractions.

Example: there's = there is

Use the Answer Box below to help you find the right word.

1. hadn't_____

2. who're _____

3. here's_____

4. I'm _____

5. who's _____

6. they'll _____

7. I'd_____

8. could've _____

9. isn't _____

10. they're _____

Answer Box

they will	you are	that is
do not	I would	let us
we would	could have	you have
he will	they are	is not
who are	here is	had not
has not	who is	I am

Name _____ Date _____

Lesson 6b: More Contractions

Directions: Write the contraction for the following two words.

Example: would not = wouldn't

1. what would _____

2. they have _____

3. there is _____

4. I am _____

5. there would _____

6. we are _____

7. does not _____

8. she will _____

9. are not _____

10. might have _____

Answer Box

there'll	we're	would've
we're	doesn't	she'll
we've	aren't	who'll
might've	what's	who'd
there's	what'd	they've
you'd	I'm	who're
shouldn't	she's	there'd

Name _____ Date _____

Lesson 7a: Number Prefixes

Siblings Born at the Same Tme	Groups of Musicians	Housing Units	Geometric Figures
_____	_____	single	line
twins	duet	duplex	angle
triplets	trio	triplex	triangle
quadruplets	quartet	quadruplex	quadrangle
quintuplets	quintet		
sextuplets	sextet		
septuplets	septet		
octuplets	octet		

Directions: Using the table above, write in the proper word.

Example: three siblings = triplets

1. two siblings _____

2. eight musicians _____

3. two housing units _____

4. three-sided figure _____

5. five siblings _____

6. six musicians_____

7. six siblings_____

8. eight siblings _____

9. five musicians _____

10. four housing units _____

Name _____ Date _____

Lesson 7b: More Number Prefixes

Siblings Born at the Same Tme	Groups of Musicians	Housing Units	Geometric Figures
————	————	single	line
twins	duet	duplex	angle
triplets	trio	triplex	triangle
quadruplets	quartet	quadruplex	quadrangle
quintuplets	quintet		
sextuplets	sextet		
septuplets	septet		
octuplets	octet		

Directions: Using the table above, translate the word into siblings, groups (musicians), housing units, or geometric figures.

Example: quartet = four musicians.

1. duet _____

2. twin _____

3. triplex_____

4. quadrangle _____

5. octuplets _____

6. quadruplets _____

7. trio _____

8. quintet _____

9. septuplets _____

10. septet_____

Name _____ Date _____

Lesson 8a: Measurement

Here is the measurement system used in the United States. We used to call it the English system because we got it from England, but the English have now switched to the metric system.

Length	Weight	Liquid
1 foot = 12 inches	1 pound = 16 ounces	1 cup = 8 ounces
1 yard = 36 inches	1 ton = 2,000 pounds	1 pint = 2 cups
1 yard = 3 feet		1 quart = 2 pints
1 mile = 5,280 feet		1 gallon = 4 quarts

Directions: Using the table above, write the equivalent.

Example: 1 foot = 12 inches

1. 1 mile_____

2. 3 feet _____

3. 1 cup _____

4. 2 cups _____

5. 1 gallon _____

6. 1 ton _____

7. 1 quart_____

8. 1 pound _____

9. 36 inches_____

10. 16 ounces _____

Name _____ Date _____

Lesson 8b: More Measurement

The metric system is used in science all over the world, including the United States. It is also used in Europe and in many countries as the only measurement system.

Length	Weight	Liquid
1 centimeter = 10 millimeters	1 gram = 1,000 milligrams	1 liter = 1,000 milliliters
1 meter = 100 centimeters	1 kilogram = 1,000 grams	1 kiloliter = 1,000 liters
1 kilometer = 1,000 meters	1 metric ton = 1,000 kilograms	

(**Note on equivalents:** 1 meter = 3.3 feet; 1 liter = 1.06 quarts; 1 kilogram = 2.2 pounds)

Directions: Using the table above, write the equivalent.

Example: 1 meter = 100 centimeters

1. 1 kilometer_____

2. 10 millimeters _____

3. 1 liter _____

4. 1 kilogram _____

5. 1,000 liters_____

6. 1 metric ton _____

7. 1,000 meters _____

8. 1 kiloliter _____

9. 1,000 milligrams _____

10. 10 milliliters _____

Review Quizzes

You can look back at the lesson if you are stuck or can't spell the words correctly, but first try to give the answer without looking back.

Lesson 5a Review: Calendar Words

Directions: Write the Greek, Roman, or Norse/Teutonic origin for the following calendar words.

Example: Vulcan, the Roman god of fire, gives us the word "volcano."

1. August _____

2. May _____

3. January _____

4. September _____

5. February _____

6. July _____

7. Wednesday _____

8. Friday _____

9. Thursday _____

10. November _____

- -

Lesson 5b Review: More Calendar Words

Directions: Pick the term taken from the ancient Greek, Roman, or Norse/Teutonic that we use today.

Example: Ceres, a Roman goddess of agriculture, gives us the word "cereal."

1. Octo (eight) _____

2. Decem (ten) _____

3. Aprilis (opening) _____

4. Mars, god of war _____

5. Juno, goddess of marriage _____

6. Tiw's day _____

7. The moon's day _____

8. Saturn's day _____

9. The sun's day _____

10. Julius Caesar_____

Review Quizzes *(cont.)*

You can look back at the lesson if you are stuck or can't spell the words correctly, but first try to give the answer without looking back.

Lesson 6a Review: Contractions

Directions: Write the contractions for the following two words.

Example: would not = wouldn't

1. we are _____

2. does not _____

3. she will _____

4. are not _____

5. might have _____

6. what would _____

7. they have _____

8. there is _____

9. I am _____

10. there would _____

- -

Lesson 6b Review: More Contractions

Directions: Write out the full meaning of the following contractions.

Example: there's = there is

1. they'll _____

2. I'd _____

3. could've _____

4. isn't _____

5. they're _____

6. hadn't _____

7. who're _____

8. here's _____

9. I'm _____

10. who's _____

Review Quizzes *(cont.)*

You can look back at the lesson if you are stuck or can't spell the words correctly, but first try to give the answer without looking back.

Lesson 7a Review: Number Prefixes

Directions: Translate the word into siblings, groups (musicians), or geometric figures.

Example: quartet = four musicians

1. quadruplets _____

2. trio _____

3. quintet _____

4. septuplets _____

5. septet_____

6. duet _____

7. twins _____

8. triplex_____

9. quadrangle _____

10. octuplets _____

- -

Lesson 7b Review: More Number Prefixes

Directions: Write in the proper word for the following descriptions.

Example: three siblings = triplets

1. six musicians_____

2. six siblings_____

3. eight siblings _____

4. five musicians _____

5. four housing units _____

6. two siblings _____

7. eight musicians _____

8. two housing units _____

9. three-sided figure _____

10. five siblings _____

Review Quizzes *(cont.)*

You can look back at the lesson if you are stuck or can't spell the words correctly, but first try to give the answer without looking back.

Lesson 8a Review: Measurement

Directions: Write the equivalent of the metric amount.

Example: 1 meter = 100 centimeters

1. 1 metric ton _____

2. 1,000 meters _____

3. 1 kiloliter _____

4. 1,000 milligrams _____

5. 1,000 milliliters _____

6. 1 kilometer_____

7. 10 millimeters _____

8. 1 liter _____

9. 1 kilogram _____

10. 1,000 liters_____

- -

Lesson 8b Review: More Measurement

Directions: Write the equivalent for the measurement below.

Example: 1 foot = 12 inches

1. 1 ton _____

2. 1 quart_____

3. 1 pound _____

4. 36 inches_____

5. 16 ounces _____

6. 1 mile_____

7. 3 feet _____

8. 1 cup _____

9. 2 cups _____

10. 1 gallon _____

Answer Key

Lesson 5

A: Calendar Words (page 18)

1. Tuesday
2. Monday
3. Saturday
4. Sunday
5. July
6. October
7. December
8. April
9. March
10. June

B: More Calendar Words (page 19)

1. Julius Caesar
2. Woden's day
3. Fria's day
4. Thor's day
5. novem
6. Augustus Caesar
7. Roman goddess Maia
8. Roman god Janus
9. septem
10. februa

Lesson 6

A: Contractions (page 20)

1. had not
2. who are
3. here is
4. I am
5. who is
6. they will
7. I would
8. could have
9. is not
10. they are

B: More Contractions (page 21)

1. what'd
2. they've
3. there's
4. I'm
5. there'd
6. we're
7. doesn't
8. she'll
9. aren't
10. might've

Lesson 7

A: Number Prefixes (page 22)

1. twins
2. octet
3. duplex
4. triangle
5. quintuplets
6. sextet
7. sextuplets
8. octuplets
9. quintet
10. quadruplex

B: More Number Prefixes (page 23)

1. two musicians
2. two siblings
3. three housing units
4. four-sided figure
5. eight siblings
6. four siblings
7. three musicians
8. five musicians
9. seven siblings
10. seven musicians

Lesson 8

A: Measurement (page 24)

1. 5,280 feet
2. 1 yard
3. 8 ounces
4. 1 pint
5. 4 quarts
6. 2,000 pounds
7. 2 pints
8. 16 ounces
9. 1 yard
10. 1 pound

B: More Measurement (page 25)

1. 1,000 meters
2. 1 centimeter
3. 1,000 milliliters
4. 1,000 grams
5. 1 kiloliter
6. 1,000 kilograms
7. 1 kilometer
8. 1,000 liters
9. 1 gram
10. 1 centimeter

Answer Key *(cont.)*

Lesson 5 Review

A: Calendar Words (page 26)

1. Augustus Caesar
2. Roman goddess Maia
3. Roman god Janus
4. septem (seven)
5. februa, Roman feast of purification
6. Julius Caesar
7. Woden's day
8. Fria's day
9. Thor's day
10. novem (nine)

B: More Calendar Words (page 26)

1. October
2. December
3. April
4. March
5. June
6. Tuesday
7. Monday
8. Saturday
9. Sunday
10. July

Lesson 6 Review

A: Contractions (page 27)

1. we're
2. doesn't
3. she'll
4. aren't
5. might've
6. what'd
7. they've
8. there's
9. I'm
10. there'd

B: More Contractions (page 27)

1. they will
2. I would
3. could have
4. is not
5. they are
6. had not
7. who are
8. here is
9. I am
10. who is

Lesson 7 Review

A: Number Prefixes (page 28)

1. four siblings
2. three musicians
3. five musicians
4. seven siblings
5. seven musicians
6. two musicians
7. two siblings
8. three housing units
9. four-sided figure
10. eight siblings

B: More Number Prefixes (page 28)

1. sextet
2. sextuplets
3. octuplets
4. quintet
5. quadruplex
6. twins
7. octet
8. duplex
9. triangle
10. quintuplets

Lesson 8 Review

A: Measurement (page 29)

1. 1,000 kilograms
2. 1 kilometer
3. 1,000 liters
4. 1 gram
5. 1 liter
6. 1,000 meters
7. 1 centimeter
8. 1,000 milliliters
9. 1,000 grams
10. 1 kiloliter

B: More Measurement (page 29)

1. 2,000 pounds
2. 2 pints
3. 16 ounces
4. 1 yard
5. 1 pound
6. 5,280 feet
7. 1 yard
8. 8 ounces
9. 1 pint
10. 4 quarts

© Teacher Created Materials, Inc.   31   #2765 Vocabulary Fun

Name _____ Date _____

Lesson 9a: Onomatopoeia

Onomatopoeia words are words borrowed from sounds, resembling the actual sound to which they refer.

Directions: Select the word that relates to the sound.

Example: boom = thunder

You can select your answer from the Answer Box below.

1. quack_____

2. bark _____

3. ding dong _____

4. howl_____

5. moo _____

6. roar _____

7. snap_____

8. drip _____

9. honk_____

10. bang _____

Answer Box

hen	brook	squeal
donkey	tired person	growl
click	crack	hiss
small bird	duck	dog
clatter	bell	burp
lion	wolf	cow
slurp	fizz	breaking twig
goose	small gun	leaking faucet
big gong	rusty door	thunder

Name _____ Date _____

Lesson 9b: More Onomatopoeia

Directions: Select the "sound" related to each word.

Example: silly child = giggle

1. cat _____

2. phone _____

3. clock _____

4. auto accident _____

5. sneeze _____

6. dog drinking water _____

7. horse hooves _____

8. bee _____

9. tearing cloth _____

10. pig _____

Answer Box

hen	brook	rusty door
donkey	tired person	squeal
click	buzz	growl
clip clop	crack	hiss
small bird	clatter	oink oink
rip	burp	moan
ring	slurp	meow
crash	tick tock	fizz
big gong	kerchoo	thunder

Name _____ Date _____

Lesson 10a: Common Roots

Knowing the root of a word oftentimes helps you know what the word means. Look at the roots in the Root Box below before putting two of them together to make a word that matches the definition.

Directions: Select the words described by the definition.

Example: fear of water (aqua) = aquaphobia (aqua + phobia).

1. fear of dogs _____

2. study of minerals_____

3. killing of insects_____

4. fear of high places _____

5. fear of enclosed spaces _____

6. study of the earth _____

7. study of birds_____

8. recorded sound _____

9. picture _____

10. story of a life _____

Answer Box

xeno = strangers	zoo = animals	phono = sound
geo = earth	auto = self	cyno = dogs
acro = high	pyro = fire	psych = mind
ornith = birds	claustro = enclosed	tele = far
photo = light	herbi = plants	-graph = write
bio = life	necro = death	-ology = science of, study of
insecti = insects	pharma = drugs	-cide = killing of
mineral = minerals	pesti = pests	-phobia = fear of
aqua = water	socio = society	

Name _____ Date _____

Lesson 10b: More Common Roots

Directions: Use the Answer Box below to write the definition for the words based on the roots "-cide," "-phobia," "-ology," or "-graph."

Example: sociology = study of society

1. herbicide _____

2. pesticide _____

3. pyrophobia_____

4. xenophobia _____

5. aquaphobia _____

6. biology_____

7. psychology _____

8. zoology _____

9. telegraph _____

10. autograph _____

Answer Box

xeno = strangers	zoo = animals	phono = sound
geo = earth	auto = self	cyno = dogs
acro = high	pyro = fire	psych = mind
ornith = birds	claustro = enclosed	tele = far
photo = light	herbi = plants	-graph = write
bio = life	necro = death	-ology = science of, study of
insecti = insects	pharma = drugs	-cide = killing of
mineral = minerals	pesti = pests	-phobia = fear of
aqua = water	socio = society	

Name _____ Date _____

Lesson 11a: States and Abbreviations

State Box

Alabama	AL	Louisiana	LA	Ohio	OH
Alaska	AK	Maine	ME	Oklahoma	OK
Arizona	AZ	Maryland	MD	Oregon	OR
Arkansas	AR	Massachusetts	MA	Pennsylvania	PA
California	CA	Michigan	MI	Rhode Island	RI
Colorado	CO	Minnesota	MN	South Carolina	SC
Connecticut	CT	Mississippi	MS	South Dakota	SD
Delaware	DE	Missouri	MO	Tennessee	TN
Florida	FL	Montana	MT	Texas	TX
Georgia	GA	Nebraska	NE	Utah	UT
Hawaii	HI	Nevada	NV	Vermont	VT
Idaho	ID	New Hampshire	NH	Virginia	VA
Illinois	IL	New Jersey	NJ	Washington	WA
Indiana	IN	New Mexico	NM	West Virginia	WV
Iowa	IA	New York	NY	Wisconsin	WI
Kansas	KS	North Carolina	NC	Wyoming	WY
Kentucky	KY	North Dakota	ND		

Directions: Using the State Box above, write the postal abbreviation for each state.

1. Maine_____

2. Alabama _____

3. Idaho _____

4. Minnesota _____

5. South Dakota_____

6. Vermont_____

7. Alaska _____

8. Illinois _____

9. Mississippi_____

10. Tennessee_____

11. Arizona _____

12. Georgia _____

36

Name _____ Date _____

Lesson 11b: More States and Abbreviations

State Box

Alabama	AL	Louisiana	LA	Ohio	OH
Alaska	AK	Maine	ME	Oklahoma	OK
Arizona	AZ	Maryland	MD	Oregon	OR
Arkansas	AR	Massachusetts	MA	Pennsylvania	PA
California	CA	Michigan	MI	Rhode Island	RI
Colorado	CO	Minnesota	MN	South Carolina	SC
Connecticut	CT	Mississippi	MS	South Dakota	SD
Delaware	DE	Missouri	MO	Tennessee	TN
Florida	FL	Montana	MT	Texas	TX
Georgia	GA	Nebraska	NE	Utah	UT
Hawaii	HI	Nevada	NV	Vermont	VT
Idaho	ID	New Hampshire	NH	Virginia	VA
Illinois	IL	New Jersey	NJ	Washington	WA
Indiana	IN	New Mexico	NM	West Virginia	WV
Iowa	IA	New York	NY	Wisconsin	WI
Kansas	KS	North Carolina	NC	Wyoming	WY
Kentucky	KY	North Dakota	ND		

Directions: Using the State Box above, write the state for each postal abbreviation.

Example: CO = Colorado

1. IN _____

2. MO _____

3. TX _____

4. AR _____

5. IA _____

6. KY _____

7. MT _____

8. UT _____

9. CA _____

10. KS _____

11. NE _____

12. NV _____

Name _____ Date _____

Lesson 12a: States and Abbreviations

Directions: Using the map on this page, write the postal abbreviations for each state.

Example: Massachusetts = MA

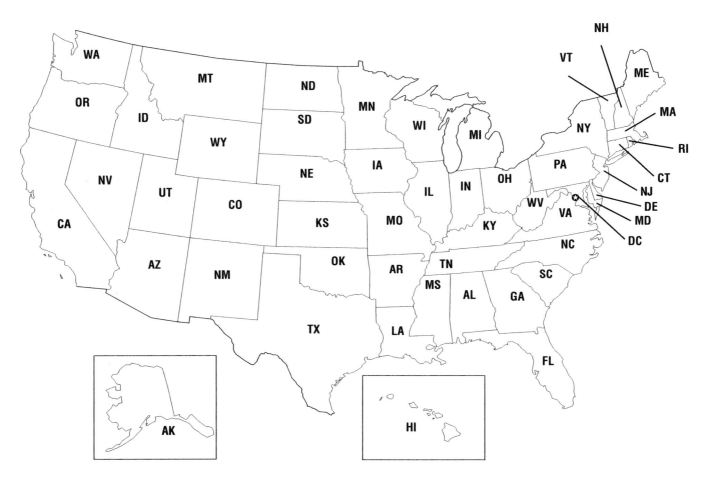

1. Connecticut _____

2. Louisiana _____

3. New Hampshire_____

4. Virginia _____

5. Delaware _____

6. New Jersey _____

7. Washington _____

8. New Mexico_____

9. West Virginia _____

10. Florida _____

11. Maryland _____

12. New York _____

Name _____ Date _____

Lesson 12b: More States and Abbreviations

Directions: Using the map on this page, write the state for each postal abbreviation.

Example: MA = Massachusetts

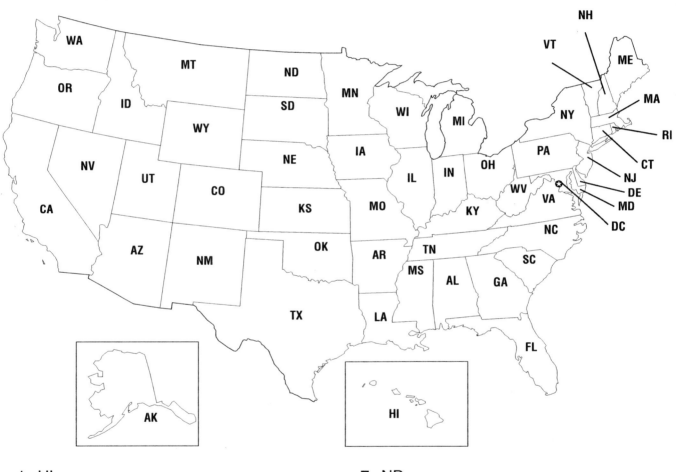

1. HI_____

2. MI _____

3. SC _____

4. WY_____

5. NC_____

6. WI _____

7. ND _____

8. RI_____

9. OH_____

10. PA _____

11. OK_____

12. OR_____

Review Quiz

You can look back at the lesson if you are stuck or can't spell the words correctly, but first try to give the answer without looking back.

Lesson 9a Review: Onomatopoeia

Directions: Select the "sound" related to each word.

Example: silly child = giggle

1. dog drinking water_____

2. horse hooves_____

3. bee _____

4. tearing cloth_____

5. pig _____

6. cat _____

7. phone _____

8. clock _____

9. auto accident_____

10. sneeze_____

- -

Lesson 9b Review: More Onomatopoeia

Directions: Select the word that relates to the sound.

Example: boom = thunder

1. roar _____

2. snap_____

3. drip _____

4. honk_____

5. bang _____

6. quack_____

7. bark _____

8. ding dong _____

9. howl_____

10. moo _____

Review Quiz *(cont.)*

You can look back at the lesson if you are stuck or can't spell the words correctly, but first try to give the answer without looking back.

Lesson 10a Review: Common Roots

Directions: Write the definition for the words based on the roots "-cide," "-phobia," "-ology," or "-graph."

Example: Sociology is the study of society.

1. biology _____

2. psychology _____

3. zoology _____

4. telegraph _____

5. autograph _____

6. herbicide _____

7. pesticide _____

8. pyrophobia _____

9. xenophobia _____

10. aquaphobia _____

- -

Lesson 10b: More Common Roots

Directions: Select the word described by the definition.

Example: Fear of water (aqua) is called aquaphobia.

1. study of the earth _____

2. science of birds _____

3. science of drugs _____

4. picture (graph) _____

5. written story of a life _____

6. fear of dogs _____

7. study of minerals _____

8. killing of insects _____

9. fear of high places _____

10. fear of enclosed spaces _____

Review Quiz *(cont.)*

You can look back at the lesson if you are stuck or can't spell the words correctly, but first try to give the answer without looking back.

Lesson 11a Review: States and Abbreviations

Directions: Write the name of the state next to its corresponding postal abbreviation.

Example: WY = Wyoming

1. MT _____

2. UT _____

3. CA _____

4. KS _____

5. NE _____

6. NV _____

7. IN _____

8. MO _____

9. TX _____

10. AR _____

11. IA _____

12. KY _____

- -

Lesson 11b Review: More States and Abbreviations

Directions: Write the postal abbreviation next to its corresponding state name.

1. Alaska _____

2. Illinois _____

3. Mississippi _____

4. Tennessee _____

5. Arizona _____

6. Georgia _____

7. Maine _____

8. Alabama _____

9. Idaho _____

10. Minnesota _____

11. South Dakota _____

12. Vermont _____

Review Quiz *(cont.)*

You can look back at the lesson if you are stuck or can't spell the words correctly, but first try to give the answer without looking back.

Lesson 12a Review: States and Abbreviations

Directions: Write the name of the state next to its corresponding postal abbreviation.

Example: MA = Massachusetts

1. ND _____

2. RI _____

3. OH _____

4. PA _____

5. OK _____

6. OR _____

7. HI _____

8. MI _____

9. SC _____

10. WY _____

11. NC _____

12. WI _____

Lesson 12b Review: More States and Abbreviations

Directions: Write the postal abbreviation next to its corresponding state name.

Example: Massachusetts = MA

1. Washington _____

2. New Mexico _____

3. West Virginia _____

4. Florida _____

5. Maryland _____

6. New York _____

7. Connecticut _____

8. Louisiana _____

9. New Hampshire _____

10. Virginia _____

11. Delaware _____

12. New Jersey _____

Answer Key

Lesson 9

A: Onomatopoeia (page 32)
1. duck
2. dog
3. bell
4. wolf
5. cow
6. lion
7. breaking twig
8. leaking faucet
9. goose
10. small gun

B: More Onomatopoeia (page 33
1. meow
2. ring
3. tick tock
4. crash
5. kerchoo
6. slurp
7. clip clop
8. buzz
9. rip
10. oink oink

Lesson 10

A: Common Roots (page 34)
1. cynophobia
2. mineralogy
3. insecticide
4. acrophobia
5. claustrophobia
6. geology
7. ornithology
8. phonograph
9. photograph
10. biography

B: More Common Roots (page 35)
1. killing of plants
2. killing of pests
3. fear of fire
4. fear of strangers
5. fear of water
6. study of living things
7. study of the mind
8. study of animals
9. (far) sends writing
10. (self) written name

Lesson 11

A: States and Abbreviations (page 36)
1. ME
2. AL
3. ID
4. MN
5. SD
6. VT
7. AK
8. IL
9. MS
10. TN
11. AZ
12. GA

B: More States and Abbreviations (page 37)
1. Indiana
2. Missouri
3. Texas
4. Arizona
5. Iowa
6. Kentucky
7. Montana
8. Utah
9. California
10. Kansas
11. Nebraska
12. Nevada

Lesson 12

A: States and Abbreviations (page 38)
1. CT
2. LA
3. NH
4. VA
5. DE
6. NJ
7. WA
8. NM
9. WV
10. FL
11. MD
12. NY

B: More States and Abbreviations (page 39)
1. Hawaii
2. Michigan
3. South Carolina
4. Wyoming
5. North Carolina
6. Wisconsin
7. North Dakota
8. Rhode Island
9. Ohio
10. Pennsylvania
11. Oklahoma
12. Oregon

Lesson 11a: States and Abbreviations

State Box

Alabama	AL	Louisiana	LA	Ohio	OH
Alaska	AK	Maine	ME	Oklahoma	OK
Arizona	AZ	Maryland	MD	Oregon	OR
Arkansas	AR	Massachusetts	MA	Pennsylvania	PA
California	CA	Michigan	MI	Rhode Island	RI
Colorado	CO	Minnesota	MN	South Carolina	SC
Connecticut	CT	Mississippi	MS	South Dakota	SD
Delaware	DE	Missouri	MO	Tennessee	TN
Florida	FL	Montana	MT	Texas	TX
Georgia	GA	Nebraska	NE	Utah	UT
Hawaii	HI	Nevada	NV	Vermont	VT
Idaho	ID	New Hampshire	NH	Virginia	VA
Illinois	IL	New Jersey	NJ	Washington	WA
Indiana	IN	New Mexico	NM	West Virginia	WV
Iowa	IA	New York	NY	Wisconsin	WI
Kansas	KS	North Carolina	NC	Wyoming	WY
Kentucky	KY	North Dakota	ND		

Directions: Using the State Box above, write the postal abbreviation for each state.

1. Maine _____   7. Alaska _____
2. Alabama _____   8. Illinois _____
3. Idaho _____   9. Mississippi _____

Lesson

Alabama	AL
Alaska	AK
Arizona	AZ
Arkansas	AR
California	CA
Colorado	CO
Connecticut	CT
Delaware	DE
Florida	FL
Georgia	GA
Hawaii	HI
Idaho	ID
Illinois	IL
Indiana	IN
Iowa	IA
Kansas	KS
Kentucky	KY

Directions: Using the State Bo

Example: CO = Colorado

1. IN _____
2. MO _____
3. TX _____

Answer Key *(cont.)*

Lesson 9 Review

A: Onomatopoeia (page 40)
1. slurp
2. clip clop
3. buzz
4. rip
5. oink oink
6. meow
7. ring
8. tick tock
9. crash
10. kerchoo

B: More Onomatopoeia (page 40)
1. lion
2. breaking twig
3. leaking faucet
4. goose
5. small gun
6. duck
7. dog
8. bell
9. wolf
10. cow

Lesson 10 Review

A: Common Roots (page 41)
1. study of living things
2. study of the mind
3. study of animals
4. (far) sends writing
5. (self) written name
6. killing of plants
7. killing of pests
8. fear of fire
9. fear of strangers
10. fear of water

B: More Common Roots (page 41)
1. geology
2. ornithology
3. pharmacology
4. photograph
5. biography
6. cynophobia
7. mineralogy
8. insecticide
9. acrophobia
10. claustrophobia

Lesson 11 Review

A: States and Abbreviations (page 42)
1. Montana
2. Utah
3. California
4. Kansas
5. Nebraska
6. Nevada
7. Indiana
8. Missouri
9. Texas
10. Arkansas
11. Iowa
12. Kentucky

B: More States and Abbreviations (page 42)
1. AK
2. IL
3. MS
4. TN
5. AZ
6. GA
7. ME
8. AL
9. ID
10. MN
11. SD
12. VT

Lesson 12 Review

A: States and Abbreviations (page 43)
1. North Dakota
2. Rhode Island
3. Ohio
4. Pennsylvania
5. Oklahoma
6. Oregon
7. Hawaii
8. Michigan
9. South Carolina
10. Wyoming
11. North Carolina
12. Wisconsin

B: More States and Abbreviations (page 43)
1. WA
2. NM
3. WV
4. FL
5. MD
6. NY
7. CT
8. LA
9. NH
10. VA
11. DE
12. NJ

Name _____ Date _____

Final Drill

Unit I

Give a clipped word for each of these.

1. necktie _____ 2. limousine _____

Give the full word for these clipped words.

3. photo _____ 4. gym _____

Give the portmanteau word for each of the following two words.

5. motor + hotel _____ 6. twist + whirl _____

Give the two words that have been blended together.

7. flare _____ 8. hi-fi _____

Give the acronym or abbreviation for each of the following.

9. Mind your own business _____ 10. Cash on delivery _____

Give the words for the initials in each of the following examples.

11. TV _____ 12. VIP _____

Give the word associated with the famous name.

13. Louis Pasteur _____ 14. John Stetson _____

Give the person's name associated with the word.

15. Ferris wheel _____ 16. valentine _____

Answers

Teacher Instructions: Fold this section under before photocopying this page for students.
1. tie 2. limo 3. photograph 4. gymnasium 5. motel 6. twirl 7. flame + glare 8. high + fidelity
9. MYOB 10. COD 11. television 12. very important person 13. pasteurize 14. stetson 15. G. M.
Ferris 16. St. Valentine

Name _____ Date _____

Final Drill *(cont.)*

Unit II

Give the word taken from mythlology that we use today.

17. decem _____ 18. Saturn's day _____

Give the mythological origin for the following words we use today.

19. January _____ 20. July _____

Give the two words combined for the contractions.

21. here's _____ 22. isn't _____

Give the contractions for the two words.

23. might have _____ 24. there would _____

Give the number prefix word for each of the word groups.

25. two housing units _____ 26. six siblings _____

Give the word group that describes each of the number prefix words.

27. duet _____ 28. quadrangle _____

Give the English/U.S. system measurement.

29. 1 pound _____ 30. 1 gallon _____

Give the metric system measurement.

31. 1,000 meters _____ 32. 1 liter _____

- -

Answers

Teacher Instructions: Fold this section under before photocopying this page for students.
17. December 18. Saturday 19. Janus 20. Julius Caesar 21. here + is 22. is + not 23. might've
24. there'd 25. duplex 26. sextuplets 27. two musicians 28. four-sided geometric figure
29. 16 ounces 30. 4 quarts 31. 1 kilometer 32. 1,000 milliliters

Name _____ Date _____

Final Drill *(cont.)*

Unit III

Give the word that relates to the sound.

33. moo _____ 34. quack _____

Give the onomatopoeia sound word that relates to each word.

35. bee _____ 36. sneeze _____

Give the root word described by the definition.

37. fear of high places _____ 38. study of the earth _____

Give the definition for the root word.

39. autograph _____ 40. psychology _____

Give the postal abbreviation for each state.

41. Idaho _____ 42. Tennessee _____

Give the state for each postal abbreviation.

43. CA _____ 44. TX _____

Give the postal abbreviation for each state.

45. Florida _____ 46. New Jersey _____

Give the state for each postal abbreviation.

47. MI _____ 48. OH _____

- -

Answers

Teacher Instructions: Fold this section under before photocopying this page for students.
33. cow 34. duck 35. buzz 36. kerchoo 37. acrophobia 38. geology 39. self written 40. study of the mind 41. ID 42. TN 43. California 44. Texas 45. FL 46. NJ 47. Michigan 48. Ohio